mostly summer
by Louise Weld

Copyright © 2024 Louise Gwathmey Weld

All rights reserved. This book was made with love. For information on purchasing this book in bulk for educational or promotional purposes please contact the publisher at **freeversepublishing@gmail.com** or visit **freeversepress.com.**

Obviously: No part of this book may be reproduced, distributed, or transmitted in any form or by any means, including photocopying, recording, or other electronic or mechanical methods, without the prior written permission of the publisher, except in the case of brief quotations embodied in critical reviews and certain other noncommercial uses permitted by copyright law. Cool?

ISBN: 979-8-9871632-2-1

Design by Marcus Amaker

Printed in the United States of America.
First printing edition 2024.

Published by Free Verse Press
Free Verse, LLC
North Charleston, South Carolina
freeversepress.com

Table of contents

Fall

Wild night
The visit of the red tailed hawk
Shrimping on Marvin and Bubba's dock
Mrs. Bowen crosses the bar
Hurricane warnings

Winter

Bus Stop on Line Street
Winter Woods
Mr. Johnson's Funeral
Givhans Ferry

Spring

Undoing
Reflected Glory
Neighborhood Rooster
Sullivans Island
The Black Skimmer
Tidal Creek
Death of the Yellow-Rumped Warbler

Summer

A Rash of Minnows
Creek Evening
Carolina Wren
Summer Storm
Old Woman Waking
Such a Tiny Lizard
Lunar Eclipse
The End of Summer
Reenactments
The Heron and the Redfish
Grace Notes
The Night Herons Have Taken to the Street
Bet
The Given Life
The Year SC Debated the Removal of the Confederate Flag
Blue Bird
Botany Bay Outing
I'll Fly Away

Fall

Wild night

the north wind sweeps the creek
the arthritic fingers of the live oak tremble
and lose their grip on hoards of acorns
which scuttle and bounce off surfaces.
The first bonfire of the season flings its scent in the air
and the children are everywhere in the wild night,
they call it Hide and Shriek for fear of the dark,
daring to shrink themselves into webby crevices,
afraid to look for one another, afraid not to be found,
wanting to find and be found and ecstatic in the wanting.
Breathless, they tell us that when someone stirs the fire
and a cloud of sparks blooms in the air
you can make wishes, secrets
like the wishes they are themselves, hidden in the bloom
of small bones and flesh and caution of their parents
who want the world for them, but for fear of their own dark hollows
call them in to settle them down before bedtime,
do not dare to leave them in their own unexplored territories.

The Visit of the Red Tail Hawk

In October the yard has little
left to say, begins its forlorn slump
into the contemplative season
hydrangeas, drooping and exhausted from their flouting
the grass loses its impulse to grow,
the marsh beyond the creek dulling down, brown,
and the squirrels, their nests thick in the limbs of the oak,
are having a last hoorah, picking at the mushrooms
that appeared like colonies of intruders in the yard this morning after rain.

A solitary mallard has left the creek and taken up loitering in the pool
Now the red tail hawk, a silent shadow, streaks through the damp air, then
a tumult of flapping and swooping after the duck
who promptly bottoms up, moons him, and dives deep into the pool.
The hawk retires to a tree to wait for an opportune moment
but does not take into account the offense he is to the company of squirrels
into whose territory he intrudes.

Who knew it was in us, not only to be duck, or squirrel, or hawk, but also
to startle ourselves out of our genetic predispositions
for the sake of what matters? And suddenly
the leaves are rustling, the branches tremble, the entire tree
shaken with the hissing and chattering squirrel, the wildly thrashing tail of the rodent
turned warrior, faced off against the magnificent, feathery giant.
The hawk does a reverse flap and backs away.
He lifts off and sails out of the yard. I swear I saw it with my own eyes,
a tale of Biblical proportions
In the grand scheme of things, these encounters take my breath away:
the hawk intent on his prey, the wisdom of the duck; the way the squirrel finds his voice,
the retreat of the hawk; and the mallard, surfaced
and skiing now, wing propelled back and forth across the pool
simply it seems, for the joy of flapping.

Shrimping on Marvin and Bubba's dock

The breeze lifts,
up creek a dog barking

on the edges of the inky stream egrets pick at pools
of minnows and marsh hens squawk near water popping with shrimp;

tonight I am blessed by two old men with the gift
of their salt-soft dock, the sky singing with stars,

and pluff mud dug from the steaming marsh
to squeeze and form and dip in fishmeal.

Wet-furred Sally expects her cut; she'd be happy to eat the bait balls.
she's been in the creek herself; her ears twitch at the slap of the net.

Marvin and Bubba are brothers: Marvin was born a wanderer
and drifted upstream for awhile all the way to Chicago. Tonight

he's off to the concert in town. Bubba stays alongside the creek
and listens to the seasons, says he doesn't know why Marvin likes all that music.

Bubba prefers the fugues of draining and filling tides,
the shrimp shaken out of the net popping and snapping on the dock.

Bubba, on his boat with his tools, undistracted by the years,
has no need to leave. But he tells himself, at least Marvin knows to come home

every fall when the shrimp come up creek to spawn.

Mrs. Bowen Crosses the Bar

On Howe Creek, a blue moon
swells the tide out of its creek skin

and rolls it close to her porch.
She has deplored the pollution

of the creek by developers, seen children
and grandchildren married and unmarried

and held her tongue; buried
her husband, decapitated in an accident.

When the wildlife people made her remove
the KEEP OFF signs from the sand flats

in front of her house, she summoned
all her friends to come harvest the clams

so nothing more would be stolen from her.
Did she trust the tide to keep its place?

Was she a hermit crab outgrown her shell?
Or was she snoozing on the porch

and slipped through the dream of her life
into her heart's current; and what

marvelous wonders did she see
as her body floated face down, snaking

towards the sea? They found her footprints
in the mud edge of the creek.

According to the newspaper, "The body
was fully clothed and still wearing
sunglasses."

Hurricane warnings

Waiting is itself
its own pressing humidity, wearing us down:
the need to know,
the necessary work of the unknown.
And along the Carolina coast the hunkering down
The storm briefly roars into significance as
a Category 3, dark and ominous.
The wind pressures every resisting wall,
bulges the windows, sucks
the water out of toilets
churns a trailer park into smithereens.

Just as quickly it loses steam and interest
in the present calamity
moves on, cuts a drenching path
all the way to New York state where
my son in his front yard waiting
for rain and flash floods
sees a mother deer
hears her squawk of alarm
as a coyote creeps across the grass
toward her fawn
thinks of his own daughters
asleep in their beds
tries to wrap them in his own thin air.

This is the work of poetry and religion
to be pinned down by something
in the air, a waiting, a not knowing.
And if the truth be told
a wild and upheaving wind would not be unwelcome.
Sometimes, you have decided
to make a life of the waiting, and
sometimes something like a hawk
without warning dives and snares
a piece of you, or all of you
and you are left gasping and snatching
at whatever can be salvaged
and it could be a poem
or it could be a prayer

Winter

Bus Stop on Line Street

Damp splinter of bench, this cold, grim wind
this community of believers
accustomed to waiting on someone else
to get them where they need to go.
A wild-haired prophet paces like a worried crane
and mutters, shaking his head
in an argument only he hears.
Two young women chewing gum,
both talking at the same time.
Teenagers pass around a joint.
Stuffed in neoprene so stiff he can barely stand
a toddler whines and tugs at the immoveable
shape of his grandmother. Her eyes are fixed
on another point in time: her waiting
in the warm pantry for the family to eat their dinner.
They love her cooking. Everybody does. Her church circle
is always asking for her devil's food cake. Her
own family waiting for her to bring home
the dishes of leftovers, special treats, small
gifts of money. She gives a little shudder,
notices the child is crying, picks him up
hugs him. "You hush now sweet baby,
bus coming soon."

Winter woods

Slug the forlorn fields, enter the woods
every tree on the brown hillside a somber view
of things as they now stand. Leaves sodden and slippery,
rotting the secretive creek; catastrophe of fallen oak,
black walnut bent double in a last gasp.
The wounded everywhere,
propped against their own sorrows:
great or spindly trunks; arthritic joints,
bark hanging in tatters from their bones,
the skeletal fatigue of refugees.
And among the tripping roots, the cracked and severed linden,
so many black and abandoned entrances
imply a hollowing.

It is a solitary and brittle time
to stand in the cluttered ruin;
this bleak country of mourning:
brown, brown the muted day
sorrow, sorrow the rueful branches:
lost hope, lost memory, failure to thrive, present forgetfulness.

And why shouldn't the One who came to earth to remind us
of ourselves, who now has little else but time on His hands,
why shouldn't He give us a taste of what He had to put up with?
Lost, the glitter and shimmer of the splendid green canopies
the sweet wind making a chorus of the leaves
the preening trees, squirrels and birds chitting
their claims to one another; inquisitive leaping deer,
creeping fox; provocative small violets and blinking invitations
of nests and nuts, all that can be seen and lovely, even
all that is hidden in the mossy crevices, tantalizing, from view

Oh, the shame, the grief of it! Oh broken and breaking world.
Oh necessary seasons. Oh plain sight
of His relinquishing: this mangled view,
the hands of Him who entered His own dark wood
who made of His own scarred surfaces this map of the known world;
and even in this, breeds
the warm and broody wind.

Mr. Johnson's Funeral

He stood our fresh mullet shapes on the strand,
tickled us with crosscurrents of sea oats.
We left our mothers in the lurch. We were dawn splitters,
icy cokes in our shrimp scum hands, his best
fishing girls. One summer we began to sleep in
our bodies consumed with their own ocean swells.
After that he fished with our brothers
and left it to our mothers to shingle us from what
storm we never knew.
At Saint James Church, his widow carries grief
like a bulging purse, smoothes her daughter's skirts,
cautions against the excess of tears.
His first grandchild strains to wiggle the hard pew.
A reception follows at the home. Brushed kisses.
Murmured sympathies. Firm and heartfelt handshakes. Steady
as she goes. And then, a rogue wave,
the smallest mourner, he slides down his grandfather's
banister shrieking like wind through spreaders.
There's no hushing him.

Givhans Ferry

Behold the root lacerated path
through the woods at Givhans Ferry
so many trunks and vines and branches
stunned and hesitant like they have forgotten
what they were set out to do.
There are dark holes in trunks
and gashes, and damp hollows of leaves and mold
and all under limp, chilling clouds.

Behold the stillness: no wind creak,
no distraction of leaves, no bird call, no growling squirrels.
An extravagance of silence
that inclines you to whispering
as though entering a great cathedral.

Behold scattered on the gnarly ground
bright votives of yellow jessamine
the delicate wonder of them, so glowing, so perfectly shaped,
like openings, an astonishment of carelessness, and where did they come from,
this broadcast of the scent of sun
lighting up the somber ground?

And so the jessamine in very late winter,
proffers the first hope of warm weather to come.
The brown forest poised, already predisposed to explode
into greens so fresh it will bring tears to your eyes,
But like so many things,
these fragrant beauties are laced to poison and wither at the touch
and cause their own withering;

Behold the things you tell yourself about your latest attempt to thrive or
your plans for what is just around the corner
this time it will be different, this new season.
it is the cracked branches that represent your true hollowing and leeching and
in the withering, the hope…

SPRING

Undoing

For we know that the whole creation has been groaning together… Romans 8: 22

The arrangement: I provide
housing with a view,
the grand oak, its coverings and crevices,
a yard for soaring and flitting,
your own private feeder piled high with the delectable mealy worm.
The children forbidden to intrude.
(I see you find it entirely to your liking,
bring mossy twigs, dried leaves,
fashion a settling space, and finally
you take up a position
on a dipping branch, to regard the world that
has come to hold all your imaginings)

Your part of the arrangement is simply to offer
me your pure and undiluted blue, it seems the whole sky has been pulled
down into the color of feathers. And I find myself stilled
by your watchfulness, you may have meandered
here from the center of all things created. I imagine
that you, like me, are given to the solitary. Let the blackbirds
screech and flap like banshees from the bamboo thicket.
Not for you the convocation at the company feeder,
titmice and wrens and cardinals, the feisty warblers,
doves patrolling the ground below.
Yours is the considered life, tidy, in your heart

for your little family is an eternity of hope.
I come to regard us as keepers of the known world, and to imagine
that God finds in our companionship a recollection
of his own first garden of delights, his own
pleasant plantings, love's own need to share what love creates.
But yesterday your house was flung wide open,
your nest ravaged. A snake? Raccoons? An errant child?
Am I to conclude that nothing is sacred? Nothing certain except betrayal and loss?
Ah, I had too high an opinion of my proprietary self.
Who can keep anything safe in this world?
I fasten the birdhouse shut. The view has turned

dull, unremarkable. I know myself to be cowering,
exposed: here on the porch searching for words

which are like fledglings,
their beaks wide open for food, utterly at the mercy
of this world which has cast aspersions on its own ability to provide.
Meanwhile the animals go on about their business of marking
territories and making the best of a poor situation.
A squirrel chews through screen and vinyl to deposit its cache
of broken acorns in the basket of towels on the porch.
The raccoon prowls the dock at night, tattoos the john boat with pluff mud.
Beyond the fence, beavers approach unseen from the creek,
chew and make off with the tops of three trees
whose trunks now stand in a clearing,
wood chips everywhere like flecks
of blood, scattering the ground.

Reflected Glory

On the fifth day, God breathed
out a substance of wings and webbed feet, feathers
of every hue, birds of every calling and disposition,
an extravagance of joy, including
a sense of the absurd (so testify the pelican and the spoonbill).
These days, it is not the birds themselves, but the birds
which are not birds which call to mind for me
their maker's breath still lingering in the washed and fading
lines, even in their blurring. Shattered and lovely in their
shattering, out of focus, upside down, blur of light, wind, fish
scatter, wrinkled, their true shapes just perceptible on the
creek that is sometimes not a creek,
itself beset with ambiguities:
every emptying crevice wistful, a hollowing,
every filling a mercy refracting to a new view.
The little blue sees himself floating as he searches
for food, his own reflection a hunger itself.
The fact of his hunger skitters the fish,
breaks his image into shivers of bright light,
hope substantial, dissolving, perceptible…
then we shall see face to face.   1 Corinthians 13: 12
For now we see only a reflection as in a mirror;

Neighborhood Rooster

Houses built on the sand edge of once was,
used to be the swale which halted the ocean's
proud waves, now yards fenced in and sodded, with
covenants against imagining.
On a summer morning before the heat takes hold
and wondering lowers its shades
it is no small pleasure to be awakened
by a rooster with a cackle that is all proprietary glee
for servicing his pack, his hens clucking and gleeful
when their mission is accomplished.
There is something to be said
for the irreducible force of a bird
with nothing else in mind but the sound of its own voice;
not for him the Do Not Disturb and No Trespassing
signs to let the world know your property lines.
No quieting his screech and cackle,
the air acoustical with his narcissistic racket.
Some in the neighborhood would like to shoot
the damn bird. But I say listen and be disturbed.
Listen and let your irritation rise, a tremble
to rumple the hedges of your pressed down life.
Feel it thicken your throat: a cry for the thing which
is perched on all your fences: even as you
sleep, and wake, and eat, and love, and lose, and
begin it all again the next morning, and the next.
Listen, until you fall out
of the rhythm you didn't know
was pressing you in, and rattle
the stretching day with the sound of your own crowing.
During the night some critter has gnawed a hole through
my screen porch. Even now, a loud mouthed sparrow
clings to the same screen, scratching its way in.

Sullivan's Island shrimpers

five am rumbles
humming, gangly, weather beaten
women headed for the open sea
into the final edge of the night:
silence, stars,
hazy curve of moon
Dark water parts and glitters
with a certain trailing grace.
Yawning and stretching nets
drag against singing winches
The coffee so hot it fogs the eyes.
Their lights spread across the wall
of my room, tease me awake.
And though I have wrapped myself in solid ground
I drift back into a dream of being expected
by dolphins in my own rolling wake.

The Black Skimmer

The skimmer reams the creek with his incisive jaw
parts the ragged creek: egret here,
minnows there in nervous disarray
The breeze all whimsical and fey.
He is a military bird, at war against the Fall
imprecisions and imperfections all.
He relies on straight-edged protocol.
A solitary flyer, he, his black-tipped beak
Red following mandible slices like a knife
Precise, clean cut, no doubt about his life:
Simply to catch a fish, a shrimp, an eel
Food that is, as he is, urgently real.

Tidal Creek

The current slips out
lurking birds
in the grassy sway
clamor of minnows
errant crab
shrimp sent scampering
as a spot tail lumbers
the shallows.
I've seen my children take up the same positions
establish and intrude on territories
startle at the flopping mullet
wallow in pluff mud
lift off to another flat
then circle back with an irresistible
draw to substance.
Every creek is a society of longing
herons of various sizes and shapes
the shy marsh hen, brown as mud
the great blue a loud squawker;
a raccoon come and gone
after the stream went slack,
his tracks lead to the great oaks beyond the marsh.

Death of the Yellow-Rumped Warbler

Sleep now
soft song
down swaddles you
your stillborn chirr all
the life you will know
the fluttering day
its green advances
bees beginning their slow
stagger after food
swarms of keyed up gnats
grass unfurling
under drooping cedar
you lie on straw
attended by mourners
who know you
as bright epiphany not
this too soon
too still

SUMMER

A rash of minnows

When thunder bristles
the back of summer
trees turn their leaves
upward, making petition for
tenderness.

Spanish moss clings
to the arms
of the great live oak
and catches all
her broken promises

I cannot tell
exactly when the tide
turns in the creek,
but the marsh
and the mullet know.

During thunder storms
my dog flings himself
against locked doors.
This is what I remember
about summer.

Creek Evening

soft somnolent creek time
opal slipstream
twirling hair lingers
among the worn marshes
slipping sun
slaked mosquitoes laze
over crab buoys
we are low-lidded, dreaming,
when we both see it:
the same black shape
like a human head
like a boggle head
startle the surface of the creek
then slip away, under its own volition?
Brief as a caught breath, silent as
the light slipping into night and
on the surface of things
not so much as a shrug or a ripple left
to credit to its appearing
what is it that stirs in the nether creek
to snag us by its appearing?
a crusted buoy straining to break free of its drowning?
what serpents or leviathans eddy us
towards the dreads we don't even know?
our own dark dragons surfacing and snagged
then dragged back under
on our own flinching damps
what was it? why are we whispering?

Carolina Wren

Wren, what have you done? Almost got yourself killed
going where you had no business going. Not enough for you,
the yard perking with water bugs and crickets, the tangled brush,
leaf litter, azalea thicket? And as if that weren't plenty,
bird feeder, suet and mealy worms? You and your companion,
oh the duets you sing, of trysts in the marsh and hatches and so many
chatters of children come and gone, and the simple pleasure
of coming home to nest day after day, year after year to your one true love.
Sounds like God's own paradise to me. But as is the way of things
ever since the gate slammed shut, all that we are given can be as nothing
before the sudden ravages of the outcast soul.
Presented with our own necessary hiding, we are no longer ourselves,
are obsessed with fences and closed doors, the irresistible hole in the screen.
You slip through, scratch at the leaves of the rubber plant, make
an aerial inspection of the fan, begin to notice
the porch's insufficiencies. The dog, normally content
with the confines of suburban dogdom, explodes from her dream:
the dog is crazed with longing, the polite and gentle dog
is climbing furniture and crashing into tables, traps you
in a corner. You frantic, fluttering in the most appetizing way,
crazed yourself now for what once was and never shall be.
What I rescue from the saliva slinging mouth of the dog is
finally, in the cup of my hand, wet and trembling fluff, surely
too insubstantial to bear the burden of God's grief.
I set you free. I settle the dog. I breath a sigh of relief.
Often, now, in the late afternoons you come to hunch down
high in the crook of the eaves, flank and rump a round tent, beak tuck,
head pressed against the wall, tail down. You spend the night,
you seem the very shape of regret. And when you are gone
in the morning we want to believe that we also, home and heart sick,
may be rescued from our sad proclivities, our flights of fancy,
we too delivered from the burdens of our longing, we too captured,
we too set free, the dog feels it in her bones, I know it as a breeze stirring.

Summer Storm

The day bottoms out, heat browns
the reaching plants. The marsh bends before a drouth of salt.
Even those who believe in the seasons are discouraged
by their own listlessness.
The rain we seek is neither monsoon or cat
but the spinning of memory into some small comfort
rain like the relief of light in childhood nightmares.

Tonight is forecast a band of storms
with hail the size of quarters, tongue lashing winds
the creek is still and steaming in the heat
Breeze on the skin perks the attention of gulls
drags the scent of fox across the cracking yard
Musicians hear all these discrepancies as notes,
fan out their anguish on the reeds and drums and speak their headtunes
through the disharmonies of rhythm. Poets hear the vowels of sweat
and dig wells in the clouds. Novelists are shaken by their own fictions
and write stories with no endings.

Finally, we hear the rain at night. It comes without fanfare, like sleep.
And we fall into a dream of a play in which we all have parts
but have forgotten all our lines.

Old Woman Waking

In the shingled cottage a woman older than she wants to be lies sleeping
the sleep of exhausted bone, her breath as sweet as song, her mouth open,

softly snoring. Upstairs her middle-aged son listens on the intercom to this ocean
lapping his shores in the predictable way of waves. She sighs

and mutters in her dreams. He strains to understand if she is
calling him, his own anxious mothering turning and twisting him

out of his sheets. He goes downstairs in the gray dawn,. But still she sleeps,
ebbing and flowing against the brittle hold of her ship, planked in pine and poetry. Oh yes,

she has had plenty to say to her children, about the craters they have left behind.
Old age has tuckered her womb. The sea stretches in its customary growls,

it has been roaring at the stars all night. Now dawn fades into a dreamscape. She's
a slim, shiny haired child, her skin back-lit by the moon, perched before the moment

of herself, then diving straight into black water, lighting it with the fluorescent shape
of a bird. Willets and sanderling skitter the dim shore, darting anxiously

from the paws of waves. Under the dock a heron stands alone
and silent, the soft day.

Such a Tiny Lizard

snared in a cobweb under the kitchen chair,
first I think he's dead, a trophy brought home to dinner
not yet consumed; but
he shivers at my touch.
Grandson gently extracts him from his gallows
takes him to a bush in the yard,
transfers him to a soft leaf.
Then, clearly concerned about
his grandmother's underworld,
grandson offers to clear out all the cobwebs
under my chairs. He is sixteen, stretching and pulling
against his own attachments
he believes cobwebs are a benign neglect

Little does he know
what he's getting into:
a lot more critters clinging or clung to,
hanging out, biding their time, unwilling to die,
mostly benign by nature, yet indelibly
present in this netherworld. It's why
I've left the underpinnings to their own devices.
You reach for the thing you see
and then there's a shadow just beyond
and here and there dark presences
and what comes to mind
floating in the drifty webs
with insects and dust mites and dirt are
attachments and regrets
that you've given a wide berth
believed to be dead and long gone,
but whose presences surface,
reaching, clinging, caught

Lunar Eclipse

The night stops singing midstream
over the phosphor creek.
Red simmering fury of moon,
a phantom throws his cloak
over her lustrous flesh,
then rolls away towards brighter stars.
(Old age arrives with the same
dimming, a catch in the throat,
the heart skips a beat, an altered view.)
The dolphins snort and dive.
From his cold perch the pelican leans
and clucks at the thrust down time.
A hard mercy, this darking down.
Some believe it is
the end of the world.

end of summer

Mildew is the last green vine
to grow up the sides of the house
Heat daze glazes its own surfaces
Sheets limp the line, and what
the gleaners have left is a sweet decay.
In this drench of fatigue, spiders
store their sulks in every ravelled corner
gathering the lost threads
of vainglory for their pouty webs.

Reenactments

Of Breach's Inlet on a night like no other
the Warship Housatonic rides the chill netherworld,
the sleeping crew dreams of home. The lookout
watches the dark water swelling towards land,
eyes the starless sky, and worries about a certain
edge in the air that shivers his bones, the way back home
he can feel snow coming. Under the pouting sea,
the hand driver churns closer, the crew
are sweating in the belly of the butt-headed fish.
Young Lt. Dixon and his men are used to the heat—
He's from Kentucky, a horseman until a musket ball took him
down but didn't kill him; for good luck he carries the $20 gold piece
that saved his life once already. The Hunley drives towards its enemy,
rams its stinger in the side of the giant, backs off,
and blows it up. On Sullivan's Island the rebels
stomp and cheer the lightning sky. Then dark.
The bruised sea seals its lips and refuses
to speak another word, as she settles
the righteous corpses in the burying mud.
Off Breach's Inlet, near the shipping lanes,

the USS Housatonic lies in a smash, forever in silt, her crew
gone to brood marrow for the honor of her country's bones.
But look! The Hunley rises from its grave
in the slug-mire of history. The sea is reluctant
to release its bounty of souls in barnacle and crust
but must defer to the National Geographic Society. The wounded fish
breaks clear of gravity, pulled toward heaven by cranes.
Traffic stops on the Cooper River Bridge. Bridge travellers,
girls in bikinis, tourists, politicians, reenactors,
all revel in the glistening relic. Church bells peel, whistles and horns
and shouts, cheering and weeping and babbling adorn the rising
as if it meant the turning of all their wars.

Something falls in this rising, the vast unknown
made manifest like the wrong bite of an apple,
And the trough of the harbor shifts around its wound
covering its losses. The sunken world surfaces for breath
on Queen Street, where dull-eyed young men wait
for the day to pass, smooth young girls in dreadlocks
chant to their jump ropes and tourists
in carriages pass by the housing project on their way
to the Slave Museum. Dolphins patrol the streets
on horseback looking for their confederate dead.

The Heron and the Redfish

The tipping blue heron
and the great wallowing
redfish make their way together
on an afternoon jaunt seining the creek,
they send minnows and shrimp flicking the air,
clouds of mud bloom in the water
which is receding to snails and shining mud.
The fish needs a certain amount of water
for the journey but is hunger clumsy
and slugs to a halt in a mound of pluff,
rolls over on his back
and with a giant thrashing of his tail lurches himself
back into the stream. The heron stands
back, as though skeptical of this heroic display
of floundering: its not the first time it has happened
and will not be the last interruption to their common calling.
It seems there is always a rift in the natural world
getting in the way of relationships.
He considers the narrowing channel, cuts his losses
lifts off, he's got his own instabilities, a flightiness
that has him forever looking ahead to the next curve in the creek.
Scoff if you will at my imaginings of birds and fish being
companions on the way
but I have heard it said that one day the wolf will dwell with the lamb
and the leopard lie down with the young goat
why not a foretaste of eternity in this creek also,
even in these disabled associations who
press on their way interrupted
as fiddlers scurry over the empty path of the creek,
and the furtive marsh hen tiptoes in the shadows
of all creation groaning to be set free.

grace notes

pallid creek
birds streaking down, wings sun flashed
quiver surface of creek
splash   shapes   motion
all along its edges
color stirs the water
swims creek.

now the tricolored heron strikes the water
scurries its own image:
it tiptoes along, streamers of leg trail behind it.
you watch the bird: its feathers so intricately arranged
its precise beak and claws, its blinking eyes scan the water
for fish and then
you see suggestions of bird
body bent and blurred
neck sliced into latticework
the bird so attentive to its prey
the reflection so attentive to the bird
sun and water dissolving precision into impression
vague, suggestive
but always there:
self contained, the bird itself and the business at hand
and its unconfined reflection, which chases or sidesteps or leads but
cannot escape the presence of its image maker
nor can it prevent its own dissolving

the bird does not notice its clinging beauty fading
in and out of focus with every fleck of motion
and you feel in yourself your own intentions and scatterings
you see what the water presents as bird
and its constant shadow companion
mocker of precision
how creek and bird together, without conscious intention, paint this patchy theology
of what has come to be, what can come of it, and how the heart is
stirred by loss and longing
these are a singing

The night herons have taken to the trees

they work the shadows of the creek
tip and toe the mud flats
harass the minnows
waiting, wary of the competition
as we all are when the air
has a certain anxiety to it
just the wisp of hint
of something coming
a presence creeping into the sway of light
and so they have taken to the trees.
They perch in the gnarly branches
of the twisted oak
hunched and sullen
guardians of the creek
which traces its path to the river
and then the ocean and beyond

Bet

Bet has three types of cancers now
and will allow the doctors no further invasions

of her wounded territories. Already her throat clutches
at words, her fear, which has heard all the promises

it can take, swells like a blister when she stands on it too long.
Fatigue garbles her afternoons

as if her body is asking her
to settle on the quilt of its yielded life

making its own essential region and filling it
with the warm, crescent breath of her landscapes

letting down, after a killing winter, into luxuriant spring.
Her son runs in to tell her he has caught a fish.

How big, she asks? Well, about as high as my knee,
the boy says with a smile she sinks into, feels herself rising

The given life
> *We live the given life, and not the planned.* Wendell Berry

Straddle the floating dock
for no other purpose than pitch
and sway, rise and flow of
water in cahoots with the moon.

Notice a dart of light,
back fin of a rising mullet
marsh grass bent but not giving way
twitching nose of the dog

sprawled on the salty plank. There's a man
down the creek with his dog, he's smoking, and the air
carries the scent of his own waiting; anxious,
he lights another cigarette.

The water moves at its own pace
alerts me to my own impotence, unnecessary to the life
all around me, life whose ebb and flow
do and undo me.

The night heron ignore me, the wrinkling ducks,
an alarmed egret flaps from the tree as the osprey swoops in.
The rooster screeches from across the way.
The sun strikes the edge of the marsh bank,

shining the mud. It will now begin its own warming creep
across the scene. There is a settling in
that is my unsettling, and I am grateful for it;
that this world will not let me have my own way with it.

That I cannot turn the ebb
cannot command the sun to wait a few minutes.
It is a gift to behold the water gush and suck
and see what is left clinging to surfaces

The Year South Carolina Debated the Removal of the Confederate Flag

Droughted days, millennium spring gone
gossipy and strident, a semi-tropical boil.

Pleas for food and righteousness are tabled
for sentiments of pole-high passion.
Wrinkled seersucker debates flags
and formularies, all boycotted by the NAACP.

Over the State House for all to see it is
fluttering and memorable. Prayers for guidance
are fervent but compromised, as the churches are not of one mind.
The land feels arid, disappointed. All is not well.

Colors fall out of flowers. The water table drops.
residents have taken to sinking wells in sand.
Dust chokes the lily of the day; buds crack their own stalks.

On a day fuming with the heaviness of unlubricated noons
and afternoons appears the Painted Bunting,
inspects old water scumming the bird bath. Each movement

a shock of color, painful sweetness, as in the featherings
of old, lost loves. Against this flat canvas, this scorch and bubble,
these blue green and red shimmering slashes of thirst.

Blue Bird

Green fuzz tickles the sleeping birch.
Violets press through grass, clover and mint,
cense the yard with spring.

Small feathery architect, exuberant,
lights on blue plastic covering the mower
to extract a thread of sky for his nest.

But now, dangles from this dream-stopping
gallows, wings a stiff tangle. rusted breast,
tight-beaked with the unyielded string;

ruffle of unintended, unwilling, unable
twisted neck
in this noose he would not and then

could not relinquish. I am joined
to this suspended daze, lashed
to the stillness of wings.

Botany Bay Outing

Conches and skate eggs litter the beach
salt sprung wood for the gathering
the hot white sand a glare that
squints our eyes. Up the beach,
cord grass parts
goats on the prow of a dune
eye us is a way that keeps us
near the edge of the water.
The narrow-eyed ram is taller than the rest
curving horns his beard spread
like the alarmed fan of a skunk
his manhood swings between his legs
like a censor
he rubs his head
against the flank of a certain ewe
the others trotting and
deferential follow
with benign curiosity.
They tail us for awhile
almost close enough to touch
no interest in touching
then wander off like so
many endangered visions.

Here come some Shell Collectors
all pink-legged and cheerful
matching buckets
we chat with them
but do not tell them about the goats.
The air has lost its laziness
tide turns green and cool
we set sail
beat our way upwind
bucking current frisks and jars us
unbroken questions
ride us

I'll Fly Away

Alas, oh land of whirring wings
Which lies beyond the rivers of Cush… Isaiah 18: 1

over the face of the waters,
a hovering not yet named
imagined into
a sudden notion of feathers
and then the translucent sapphire sky thickens into a joyous flapping
streaming colors, shapes dipping and curving:
the great eagles, the tiny wren, and a great array of everything in between
to each of these given
a way to defy gravity
to lift off or to soften a landing
to hide their kill from competitors
a covering for their young
a way to soar higher than the eye can see
which, in the case of humans, is exactly
what Adam and Eve did, even as the creator himself
was delighting in his feathery imaginings.
They fashioned their own set of wings, flew right of the garden,
and left all creatures pretty flighty, prone to crash landings, forever
cruising the creeks in search of home.
The young osprey tumble from their nest into waves of air
and cry out for the pleasure of soaring (so soon to be a troubling necessity).
The double belted kingfisher streaks from one
piling to the next, can't stay put for long;
his hunger propels him headlong into the creek, he's his own harpoon;
the pelican's death defying catapult stuns his prey. Their wings will bear them up
to the next violence. There is a humming
in the beating wings that forever cries lost, lost. Here I cannot stay,
squawks the great blue heron from shade of the live oak. What is it calling me?
The ibis drift in their companies from one spot to the next, dripping
and slinging mud from their frantic foragings.

Though a sweet breeze wanders over the marsh
and the creek is steady and true
the view, short or long, quivers the wings.
Who can say whether wings are a curse or a blessing? God only knows.
A little wren flies through the open door of my screen porch
makes the dog frantic with its fluttering. In order to rescue the bird I must terrify it,
capture it in my hand, feel it cling and then collapse, it is so slight
in my palm, a tiny ruffle of feathers, motionless as though expired
from fright, or resigned to the error of its ways, or perhaps it thinks
it has found its heart's true home. I stand in the open door.
And then, a stirring, as it remembers its wings.

feather

> *hope is the thing with feathers   Emily Dickinson*

lovely
as the day it came to be called feather
a sun struck wisp
snagged in a tangle of cordgrass
anchored to its own reflection
in the nonchalant creek
solitary, though designed for community
useless now, though created for flight
and for what purpose does it
retain its unsinkable beauty
cast off, frayed?
rising tide will unpin it
release it to a new direction
to drift aimless on the narrow creek
catch the eye of the beholder
evoke a certain intimacy
an impression of companionship
of lament and loveliness
to make for a wondering
where it has been
and where now still is
and is being taken
lovely

Something to be said

There is something to be said
for the view of the crab below the marsh grass,
everything leveled to the lowest common denominator.
before the creek begins
to reconsider its recent departure:
periwinkles bow the spartina
tiny snails crowd the creeping waterline
in a tide pool that will just float a crab;
a spot tail stretches and roils.
The tri-colored heron and the little blue share the mud flat,
the fidgity kingfisher, still for a time on the post above.
Life is here, its own beginnings and endings
its own warm sunning with a tolerance for ambiguity,
its own resting places. And is this what
Jesus, peering down through broad galaxies and hovering moons,
has come to from the bright contented
presence of God held to himself.

Jesus, who already had in him the inclination to become what he has made,
Jesus who already knows the inevitable
sift and silt of every tide,
Jesus full of all seeing, all knowing
Jesus, fully divine and who wanted, fully human, perhaps,
simply for a time to say: I don't know either.
Who can see what is squawking around the bend
of the dense needlerush, what intrusions to the meandering creek?
Lowdown as a crab you can't tell much of anything
about any direction and this has its advantages
in terms of attention to the shrimp flutter
in the shallows. Jesus who perhaps
wished for a moment to say to himself:
I am not the future that is coming to me.
Its true, he came to save us, to become himself
the small hope, then emptied, then rising tide.
But could it have been also simply to glimpse
the bright flash of sun through the spread wing of an ibis,
his own need for warm sun on his shoulders,
the scent of shiny pluff mud that caused his self-limiting;
to settle himself in the gleaming mud that has in it
to become a sucking grave, or a sneezing
and shaking upward bound into bones and flesh;

Before the water begins its rush to fill every emptied crevice,
just for a time, as his own humanity fills his own emptied spaces
is it his want to breathe in as well as out,
to hold his vast creative breath, his eternal significance,
just for a time and
let everything be?
Just let it all be.

The Pond

from the pond roll the course cries
of bullfrogs

shugging their deep breath over wet gut
like bass players frantically sawing a scherzo

or a company of old men
all caught by asthma during the act of sex

and determined before death or despair
to finish this symphony

poets loiter there astonished
at the efforts of nature

to speak
during the languorous pauses.

Tide Turn

Urgent, the current wrings water from every
flume and crease
of marsh. From his tower of tree,

an osprey fusses and flutters,
waits for dinner on the rising tide.
Puffs of minnows muddy the shallows

as creatures who refuse to leave stake their claims
deeper in the mud. A crab hugs the backside
of a piling for dear life. You imagine you can hear the fish

waving goodbye, the crabs shaking their fists: "Good riddance!"
And then, as though someone threw up her hands
and said, "Just go ahead, take it all!   Have it your way!"—

the tide gives its last shudder, the creek flattens to a tremble.
The breeze flutters and drops. Barnacles spurt and hiss the obituary.
A great blue priest takes his position at the edge

of the water to observe the wake. All other birds fall
silent. Only gnats stir, feisty and annoying
as distant relatives wondering about the will.

In this oblique pause are all the reversals you have
ever known. Grief, erect and short-shadowed
in the hollows, waits to sign its name.

Just when you think you can't bear any more emptying,
the oysters start spitting, tisking like women arriving to take charge:
"Cheer up, cheer up, " they cluck, "It's not the end of the world."

Minnows flicker the surfaces as the current changes
its mind. Spot tails resume their wallow
in the mud, The air stirs. The breeze begins

to take itself seriously. The osprey ruffles himself to attention
with a shrug and a shake as if to say with the utmost
condescension, "Of course, the tide has turned."

The death of Elisabeth, aged 94, after Alzheimers

Elisabeth had grown weary of weeds
and such weaknesses as indispose the mind.
For all these years a lady farmer, soft-spoken in faded cottons
living alone in a wide porched house, above a pond
where she allowed fishing every day but Sunday,.

Canada geese tame as dogs took up her invitation,
crowing their approval of her rich streams
and gleaning the reaped fields.
They say she lost a soldier in the war; midlife
she took the land as a lover and kept it with a touch

that would make men weep. Testing her own good sense,
she grew organic vegetables and herds of heavy Angus,
collected honey from her hives of bees.
She blessed the land with its own riches, and did it all
for the glory of God, until one day she forgot what

she was doing and took up farming only inside her head.
Blue-eyed, lovely Elisabeth, let her gardens go to seed.
Butterflies and bees tried to pollinate her. Birds flashed and cut
their colors before her eyes. The clay sparkled its minerals.
The weeds grew up and her heart stopped keeping time

to the seasons. Suitors in black feathers came to call.
Now the full moon backs into a dark corner. Dandelions
blow ash across her pastures. Deep in the woods
there are tree trunks filled with wild honey;
and over the pond, bluets and dancers humming, humming.

Dog and squirrel

Nose twitching her toward some prehistoric notion of herself:
for what other reason these four legs, barrel chest, straining
against the leash, willing me to go where she wants me to go—
scurry of squirrels under the giant oak.
And as I have come to feel her longing
as if it were my own, I drop the lead.

She leaps into her notion of herself, bounds uninvited into the party.
Up the trunk skitter the squirrels; she tries to follow, her legs
not designed for skittering. I grab at the leash to end this
moment of grace, this small mercy of dog being dog,
when a squirrel falls from
the tree, an inch from her nose

and she's on it, swirl of fur ball and swishing tails and paws and mouth churning
together to their inevitable end, the whole scuffle an entirely silent scream.
And I'm responsible, frantic now to grab her collar, straining against the strength of her—
is it joy? In the end, I drag her away. The matted squirrel hunkers down.
The panting dog is undone by the furry taste
of freedom. The dog no longer knows me.

The dog cannot walk a straight line, pulls this way and that, my hand a millstone
on her head, she refuses to continue on the way,
no longer willing to trot beside me mostly content with her dog reality.
And truly, I see it,
as surely as the wild knowing in my own heart
has sensed what it might have been, what it cannot do:
it seems she and I have always been an accommodation.

And now unleashed in her, a hunger that will not be satisfied
until it is satisfied. This is a grace and a hard mercy. In this
world we are not able to be who we are, but can be dragged in an instant
into a violence of longing so that we can never go back to where
we never really wanted to be, forever strain
towards the scattering squirrels.

Barking Dogs

My neighbor took early retirement
for the purposes of drink and dawdle.
She sunbathes in the nude, cuts her own grass,
casts her net for shrimp from her dock on the creek.
Watches all the tv she wants, sips a lot
of wine, preferring red for her heart.
Saves abandoned dogs who sing
for their supper while she sways
to her rock and roll. Has had more than one
husband who could not dance to her tunes.
Commiserates on Facebook
with those who have lost their pets
for whatever reason. Can work up a head
of steam about just about anything,. She's a
Gawd Dammer, knows a lot of people who are
Bastards, and she will sue the Mothers
who make her mad enough. She wonders
why her grown son bothers to go to church.
Hers is her old time religion: an eye for an eye,
no grace for the democrats and the indecisive.
The emptying and filling creek is all the truth
about life and death she needs to know;
low tide and pluff mud tender in her a brief rumination
of her losses which she knows will not last longer
than necessary. Her dogs never stop barking.

Summer ending

The exhausted garden sprawls its excesses—
    tomatoes and squash splayed

in their own blood. The crepe myrtle's drooping
    breasts are the last drink of summer

Bees pull and root at the sweetness
    and can barely fly a straight line.

Vines crackle and loosen their grip
    on the skin of the barn.

If you are discomforted
    by these soft and drowsing violences, then consider

the sudden appearance of mushrooms in their hexagonal circles
    on a morning when nothing more was expected.

The great blue

stands in the clinging pluff
in the shadows in the marsh
his stare fixed on the water, no more
urgency of motion than the tide has
all in good time, bird and tide agree.
The smaller herons
come and go, anxious to scatter the shrimp;
and in the shallows the languid redfish wallows,
sluggish roll and breech   .

For an hour or so
he rustles and preens his feathers
he curls his neck into a tangled vine
he stands for long minutes motionless,
as though he is the anchor of the marsh himself

And then he strikes
mullet is flapping and twisting in his beak and then
still alive and quivering, sucked down his long thin gullet, gone.
From the creek he takes so prim a sip
of water you imagine him pushing his chair back
from the table, touching his beak with his napkin
and asking to be excused

And that is that:
the bird's sentinel encounter,
the fish which happened along
the snatching beak; the thorough swallowing
and the concluding ripples
as the water settles back into its drift.

And then the question of what my eyes have seen and whether to declare
this economy of violence, this grasping and giving up,
to be a violation of all that is life and living,
or God's own necessary provision
a sacrifice of connection if you will,
until there is no more sacrifice required?

www.ingramcontent.com/pod-product-compliance
Lightning Source LLC
Chambersburg PA
CBHW022122090426
42743CB00008B/965